60 Love Poems in English: The Most Beautiful Collection of Poems in the World

Josyie Anifka

Table of Contents

Love over time 1

Unconditional 2

A pain in my heart 4

There is no longer any reason to fight 5

Broken heart 6

A love without barriers 8

Internal fire 10

Don't go my 12

To be able to 14

I will never forget you 16

The Noble Prince 17

Sumerian poem... 18

The fire that can do anything.................................. 19

A true love 20

That is why we love each other 22

Love and spite 23

Loyalty in you 24

Myths of love kingdom 25

Light and shadow... 28

Fears 29

I wish you... 30

Pure love... 32

He did not love me 33

Soul in sorrow... 35

In the shadows of your soul.................................... 36

What it can do.. 37

An unreal love.. 38

Distance 39

A wound in the soul 40

Sadness 41
Esperanza 42
Try 44
Fears 45
A tear of farewell 46

"I love you not only for who you are, but for who I am when I am with you."- ***Elizabeth Barrett Browning***

Copyright © Original edition
2023 by Josyie Anifka
All rights reserved

Foreword

In the silence of the night, when the heart beats strongly and the soul seeks its complement, words become verses and verses become the purest expression of love.

Imagine a place where the deepest and purest feelings are transformed into words that touch the soul and the heart. That place exists, and it is the universe of poetry. In this book, "60 Love Poems in English: The Most Beautiful Collection of Poems in the World," you will find a compilation of the most beautiful and emotional love poems ever written.

Each poem is a literary jewel that will make you feel the passion, tenderness, nostalgia, and happiness that only love can awaken.

This collection will take you on a journey through the centuries, discovering the beauty of poetry in all its manifestations. Here you will find verses that will inspire you, that will move you, and that will make you dream of true love. Get ready to be carried away by the passion of words and immerse yourself in the most sublime world of poetry. This is undoubtedly the most beautiful collection of poems in the world.

Princess Yosire

In the ancient city of souls,
lived a princess of incomparable beauty,
her name was Yosire, and her heart was beating,
in search of true and unforgettable love.
And so it was that Asirm crossed his path,
a brave and passionate man,
who promised him eternal and sincere love,
and she, without a second thought, loved him with her whole self.
He left behind a life of luxury and wealth,
and with her beloved she set out for the remote lands of Yaneh,
where they built a simple but loving home,
and lived happily regardless of shortages and sorrows.
Despite criticism and disapproval from his family,
Yosire followed her heart, and fought for her love without fear,
and although he never returned to the ancient city of souls,
their story was written in the love books with much honor.
And so, the princess of Yaneh, lived happily and loved,
in a home full of love and happiness,
proving that true love,
is stronger than any wealth or vanity.
So, if at any time you feel that love is calling you,
follow it with courage and fearlessness,
because like Princess Yosire, you too can find,
a pure and real love that fills you with happiness and love.

Two souls united

In a land full of dangers and fears,
two warriors loved each other with strength and candor,
but fate would separate them forever,
in a farewell full of pain and suffering.
He, a brave and strong warrior,
I had to leave for a distant and hostile universe,
to fight against giant and powerful beasts,
to protect his people and save precious lives.
She, a warrior with courage and determination,
he had to stay to protect his home and his nation,
but his heart was breaking into a thousand pieces,
knowing that her beloved would soon be far away.
They hugged each other tightly, their bodies trembling,
and as her tears fell, time sped up,
he was to leave and she was to stay,
in a farewell they could never forget.
A farewell kiss brought them together for the last time,
and while their bodies drifted apart, their love never died,
because true love is bigger than any universe,
and would always remain, strong and eternal, like the sun.
He fought bravely and courageously in that unknown universe,
and although he never returned, their love always remained alive,
and she protected her world with strength and passion,
knowing that her beloved would always be in her heart.

Love over time

On a night of dark sky,
two young people loved each other fervently,
and even though they knew they would soon be separated,
their love would last forever, they knew.
He, a space and time traveler,
would soon depart for another universe,
in his starship would be driven away,
to a place where dreams did not bloom.
She, with a broken heart and tears in her eyes,
I knew I would soon have to say goodbye,
but he kissed her tenderly and passionately,
promising that he would always love her, without condition.
The ship took off and she watched it depart,
knowing that his love would no longer be here,
but in his heart he kept hope,
that someday they would be together again, in a dance.
However, fate had other plans,
and he never saw her again,
but their love endured over time,
and she died with a heart full of feeling.
In a dimension where dreams do not flourish,
she waited for his return, in the eternal distance,
and although time passed and he never returned,
their love was engraved in his heart, forever, like the sun.

Unconditional

In the ancient land of the Incas,
a young warrior fell in love,
of a maiden of nobility and beauty,
that her heart with her smile conquered.
But their families would not allow it,
for she was to marry a nobleman,
and he was just a brave warrior,
with a heart of gold and noble.
Still, they vowed eternal love for each other,
on top of a mountain in the Andes,
and vowed to fight against the whole world,
to stay together forever more.
But life can be cruel sometimes,
and the war separated them for years,
and even though she was still waiting,
he was left for dead on the plains.
The pain the maiden felt,
was deeper than the abyss,
and every night I mourned his absence,
yearning with all his might for his return.
But one day the news came,
that his love had died in battle,
and his heart broke into a thousand pieces,
knowing that I would never see him again.
The maiden died shortly thereafter,
overcome by pain and sadness,
and his name was engraved on his tomb,

as a tribute to their love and beauty.
So it was with the warrior and the maiden,
lived an impossible love in the Andes,
a love that transcended time and death,
and is still legendary and great today.

A pain in my heart

Heart-rending love, pain that burns,
heart betrayed, soul in pain.
Although I still love you, I know there is no turning back,
my shattered heart would not bear any more.
The memory of your kisses and caresses makes me cry,
knowing that I am no longer the owner of your love makes me
bleed.
The pain in my soul is so intense that I would like to disappear,
but I can't forget what I once loved.
Another kissing your lips, another caressing your skin,
my broken heart cannot bear this cruel role.
I know that we are no longer one, that the love that brought us
together is gone,
but my heart still beats for you, even though it feels destroyed.
Heart-rending love, pain that burns,
heart betrayed, soul in pain.
Even though I still love you, I know it's time to go,
to leave behind this suffering, to seek a new life.

There is no longer any reason to fight

In my chest, a deep emptiness,
an open wound, a broken heart,
the pain of knowing that love is gone,
that my dreams have vanished.
I gave you my soul and my whole being,
I loved you with all my strength and desire,
but now my world is in grief,
my soul in tears, my heart in mourning.
I can't understand why you lied to me,
why did you play with my love and my existence,
Was it for pleasure or for fun?
you didn't mind making me suffer?
The pain consumes me, it wounds me inside,
tears are flowing, I can't stop them,
my body trembles, my soul is deserted,
my mind goes mad, my heart goes out.
There is no consolation for my pain and sorrow,
all that remains is to accept that love is gone,
that my world has become dark and cold,
that my heart no longer beats for you.
Thus ends my sad love story,
so my soul is broken into pieces,
all that is left to do is to move forward with courage,
knowing that love will come again.

Broken heart

In the forests of Tenochtitlan,
the cry of a man without love is heard,
who lost her maiden because she was poor and worthless,
and now she finds herself in the arms of another man, and in passion.

His heart burns in flames,
sadness consumes him,
feels the deepest pain ever felt,
of a love that was never reciprocated.
But she is the only one he loves,
can love no one else,
and see her in the arms of another being,
makes him weep heartbreakingly.
The fire in his chest burns,
seeks revenge against the emperor,
for having taken from him what he loved most,
for having taken his little love.
But he knows that revenge will not fill him,
will not return his maiden to him,
the pain is still present,
and will continue to weep in the forests of Tenochtitlan.
Sadness and heartbreak accompany him,
a broken and painful heart,
looking for a way to heal,
but knowing that their love is impossible.
In the forests of Tenochtitlan,

the cry of a man without love is heard,
who lost her maiden because she was poor and worthless,
and she now finds herself giving her heart.

A love without barriers

In the epoch of the eighteen hundred years,
two young people loved each other with great fervor,
but their love was forbidden by the emperor,
who wanted to marry her off in order to possess her love.
He, a humble young man with a noble and pure heart,
He had no wealth or titles to flaunt,
but his love for her was stronger than gold,
and would fight against the whole world to be able to love her.
She, a beautiful and brave young woman,
did not want to marry the emperor without love,
and even though he knew they would fight against him,
her heart asked her to be with the one who made her happy, without fear.
Together they fled into the night, into the darkness,
crossing rivers and mountains, in search of freedom,
but the emperor would not give up so easily,
and his army pursued them, relentlessly.
In an epic battle, they fought for their love,
he, with his sword, she, with her bow and her courage,
but despite their courage, they were defeated,
and the emperor seized them, full of hatred and rancor.
Imprisoned, they knew their end was near,
but their love was stronger than any barrier,
promised to love each other forever, no matter what,
and in their hearts they kept the hope of a reunion, someday, in eternity.
And so, on a cold, dark night,

the two young lovers died with their pure passion,
in a love that would transcend the barriers of time,
and their story would be told forever, like an epic and sublime poem.

Internal fire

Love is a fire that burns without mercy,
that consumes everything in its path,
and even if you are a being of great capacity,
he transforms you into a madman in love.
No matter how strong you are in mind,
nor how much power you have in your hands,
when love knocks on your burning door,
makes you weak and makes you more human.
Your intelligence vanishes in an instant,
your logic is lost in the nebula of desire,
and you become a crazy lover,
willing to do anything for that longing.
There are no limits to the love you feel,
nor sanity that can stop its advance,
The only thing left to do is to go with the flow,
that leads you to madness and the most intense passion.
So don't be afraid to go a little crazy,
if love knocks at your door with force,
because only then will you be able to discover the treasure,
that hides behind this immense madness.

Strong love is like a hurricane,
that devastates everything in its path without mercy,
and makes you feel like a gale,
that drags you to the most intense and unparalleled passion.
It is a fire that burns in your heart,
and consumes you to the last corner,

that makes you lose your mind,
and drives you to madness and obsession.
But despite its intensity,
can also be sweet and tender,
and fill your life with happiness,
and become an eternal being.
It is a feeling that knows no limits,
and that makes you capable of overcoming obstacles,
and fight against everything that gets in the way,
because strong love is indestructible.
So let yourself be carried away by that gale,
that takes you to the pinnacle of happiness,
and do not be afraid to give yourself without equal,
to that strong love that makes you vibrate.

Don't go my

In a world of shadows and mysteries,
where death lurks warily,
two souls loved each other madly,
no matter what fate the altitude would bring them.
She, a noble and beautiful young woman,
he, a brave warrior who fought with glory,
together they defied the gods and fate,
embracing each other in the certainty that their love was genuine.
But time never forgives,
and the disease consumed him relentlessly,
leaving the maiden in uncertainty,
and her beloved, condemned to death.
She clung to hope,
fighting with all her might for her beloved,
claiming to the heavens for their injustice,
and begging for a cure that could save him.
But death makes no exceptions,
and the time of departure came without mercy,
leaving an unbridgeable void in his heart,
and an immense pain in his soul.
So, in those dark and difficult days,
the maiden had to let her beloved go,
with a broken heart and an aching soul,
but knowing that their love would live on in his memory.
And so it was, although the years passed unhurriedly,
and life went on steadily,

the love of those two lovers in the Middle Ages,
never ceased to burn in the eternal flame of beauty.

To be able to

In the time of knights and ladies,
in a world full of bravery and exploits,
a young gentleman fell madly in love,
of a beautiful lady, with a seductive look and an intelligent mind.
He, willing to do anything for her love,
I would fight against the whole world, without fear,
and she, captivated by his courage and loyalty,
gave himself to his love, without reserve or malice.
But one day, cruel tragedy separated them,
and she was kidnapped by a ruthless enemy,
he, full of pain and despair,
vowed to find her and free her, without hesitation.
Thus began his odyssey, his tireless search,
traveling through distant lands and unimaginable dangers,
on his way, he faced monsters and dragons,
and always, in his heart, his love for his beloved beat like a song.
There was no obstacle that could stop him,
no creature that would make him turn back, no matter how terrible it might be,
he was still ahead, with his sword and shield,
and the image of his beloved, as a beacon in his world.
Along the way, he found allies and enemies,
and in every battle, he demonstrated his courage and bravery,
until finally, after years of struggle,
arrived at the castle where his beloved was a prisoner, on top of a steep and hard mountain.
There, he challenged the enemy with all his might,

and fought with him, like a lion on the hunt,
until at last, with the last thrust,
defeated the evil one and rescued his beloved.
Together, they returned home, victorious and triumphant,
and their love was stronger than any adversity,
because in their hearts, they knew they were destined,
to be together forever, in happiness and loyalty.
And so, his story became a legend,
a poem of love and courage, which transcended time and eternity,
and in the hearts of those who love with truth,
there will always be a piece of that story, of that unparalleled love, of that reality.

I will never forget you

In the cold of the night,
my heart is pounding,
feeling the sadness that consumes me,
and the pain of having lost my beloved.
On starless nights,
I remember the love we once had,
and the void left by his departure,
is a weight I can't bear.
I search in vain for an answer,
an explanation for his departure,
but all I have is silence,
and the pain of knowing it is gone.
Memories flood me,
time feels like an eternity,
and every second without it,
is a blow to the heart, a wound that does not heal.
In my loneliness I lose myself,
looking for a light to guide me,
but I find only darkness,
and the emptiness of a broken heart.
In the coldness of the night,
my heart is pounding,
feeling the sadness that consumes me,
and the pain of having lost my beloved.

The Noble Prince

There was a prince in Persia,
of noble blood and brave heart,
but his love for a pot dealer,
changed his destiny in a surprising way.
Nabia was her name, and her beauty captivated the prince,
who fell deeply in love with her,
and despite the advice and warnings of his subjects,
decided to renounce his succession as king.
His father, King Ahasuerus, could not understand,
how a prince could renounce his right to the throne,
and tried to put him in jail for disobedience,
but the prince had already departed for the distant Indies.
There, in an unknown and exotic land,
found his beloved and began a new life,
leaving behind everything he had ever known,
to be with the woman who had captivated him.
And although he never returned to his homeland and his throne,
lived happily with Nabia, his princess of pots,
and was remembered as a legendary hero,
who gave up everything for love and freedom.

Sumerian poem

Once upon a time there was a young prince,
in a faraway and enchanting kingdom,
who fell madly in love with a humble shepherdess,
and renounced his throne for his love.
She was beautiful and simple,
a flower of the field that captivated him,
and although his family did not accept this union,
he was willing to do anything for love.
The prince abandoned his wealth and power,
and went far away with his beloved shepherdess,
to live a simple and loving life,
in a place where no one could judge them.
Although life in poverty was not easy,
the prince never regretted his choice,
and became a symbol of love and sacrifice,
for all those who believe in true love.
So, if you ever feel love calling you,
remember this story of a brave prince,
who gave up everything for the love of a shepherdess,
and found happiness in a different world.

The fire that can do anything

Love is a burning fire,
that burns deep in the heart,
a flame that illuminates everything it touches,
and it feels like a sweet song.
Love is a bond that unites,
two souls in one being,
a feeling that never dies,
and that makes us believe.
Believe in the power of love,
in the strength of passion,
in the sweetness of a kiss,
and in the emotion of a song.
Love is a divine gift,
that fills us with happiness,
a force that sustains us,
and gives us the strength to move forward.
No matter what,
love will always be there,
a bright light in the darkness,
and a reason to smile.
So let yourself be carried away by love,
feel its fire in your heart,
let it fill you with passion,
and feel the happiness inside you.

A true love

In ancient Sumer,
in the realm of the great Nenrob,
lived a couple in love,
who fought for his love.
She was a beautiful maiden,
daughter of the mighty king,
and he, a humble worker,
with a heart full of faith.
Despite the differences,
their love was true,
and together they dreamed of a future,
in which they would be united forever.
But the happiness did not last long,
for King Nenrob did not accept,
daughter to marry a laborer,
and his fury was unleashed.
He ordered the death of the beloved,
and the maiden wept without ceasing,
for his love had been punished,
and she could never love again.
Sadness gripped his being,
and his heart stopped beating,
for the death of her beloved,
was the end of its existence.
Thus ended their love story,
a tragedy in ancient Sumer,
that reminds us that true love,

does not always succeed in serious life.

That is why we love each other

Unconditional love is the purest,
an all-encompassing feeling,
that with its strength makes us stronger,
and leads us to touch happiness.
But sometimes, in the way of love,
betrayal and deceit lie in wait for us,
and our soul, which thought it was happy,
is broken, wounded and without hope.
Then revenge may seem sweet,
a balm for our pain,
but its taste is bitter and ungrateful,
and leaves us with more sorrows than before.
So let's better let unconditional love,
guide us on our way to happiness,
and even if pain hurts us and betrays us,
let us remember that there is always a light at the end of the
tunnel.

Love and spite

Love and spite, two sides of the same coin,
in a game of emotions that lead us to the abyss,
where the love that once shone like a sun,
fades and dies like a flame in the wind.
The spite takes possession of our heart,
and makes us desire revenge and pain,
longing for oblivion and indifference,
that allow us to move forward without fear.
But even so, love is still present,
like a wound that has not yet healed,
a memory that hurts our souls,
and makes us doubt if he will ever come back.
So let's let go of spite and rancor,
and let love be renewed,
that the flame may burn again in our being,
and may happiness bloom again.

Loyalty in you

When love is despised,
and feelings are not reciprocated,
the heart can be heartbroken,
and sadness may seem the only destiny.
But if you are loyal to your feelings,
and maintain your dignity and integrity,
even though disappointment and contempt are our daily bread,
never lose faith in love and kindness.
Loyalty to oneself is the key,
to overcome pain and contempt,
and although the wound may take time to heal,
never lose faith in love and in your sincere heart.
Because love is a powerful force,
that can heal even the deepest wounds,
and even if it is not always reciprocated,
continues to be the light that guides us in the deepest darkness.
So don't lose hope or faith,
and always keep your heart in the right place,
because true love will always prevail,
and the scorn and disappointment will soon be forgotten.

Myths of love kingdom

In ancient times, in a distant kingdom,
there was a goddess of beauty and love,
whose heart longed to find a companion
that could match his ardor.
But love for her was not easy,
since she was an immortal goddess,
and mortals feared his power and brilliance,
and never dared to go near her.
One day, while strolling through an enchanted garden,
the goddess found a young shepherd,
whose heart was beating with an intensity,
that seemed to match the flame of his own love.
Although he knew that a love between them was impossible,
the goddess fell madly in love with the shepherd,
and together they shared moments of happiness,
that only true love can ensure.
But the king of the gods, jealous of his love,
ordered the goddess and the shepherd to separate,
and that the goddess would forget her mortal love,
and return to its place in the stellar firmament.
Despite the forced separation,
the goddess never forgot her love for the shepherd,
and its presence in the night sky,
I would always remember their love with honor.
And though the shepherd grew old and died,
his love for the goddess never waned,
and every night, when the goddess shines in the sky,

the love they shared also shines through, intense and

Light and shadow

In a world of light and shadow
where love hides among the rocks,
a cool breeze whispers in your ear,
promising a tomorrow without conflict.
Birds fly free in the sky,
singing melodies of joy and comfort,
while the brightly colored flowers
radiantly embellish the landscape.
The sun shines brightly, warming the skin,
and life flows like an endless river,
in this world where everything is possible,
and the future is full of impossible promises.
So go ahead, walk without fear,
because the road to happiness is always near,
and with every step you take, you'll be closer,
to find the love and peace you long for.

Fears

At a time when wealth was the law,
getting married was difficult without much to offer,
but for those who had only love,
finding someone was a challenge and a pain.
Money and titles were the most important,
and those without them were considered less relevant,
but love does not understand titles or wealth,
and in poor hearts there is also beauty.
So those who only had their love,
They searched endlessly for someone who understood their value,
someone who knew that true love,
is not measured by wealth or money.
And although the difficulties were many,
love always found a way to fight,
and in the end there was always someone special,
who accepted others regardless of their social status.
Because in the end, what matters most is love,
and those who have it are blessed above all value,
and although wealth can bring comfort and well-being,
true love is the one that will really make you prosper.

I wish you

Dear reader, let me inspire you,
with words that come from the heart,
I will take you on a journey of emotions,
in a world full of passion.
I will talk about eternal loves,
that transcend time and space,
of soft and tender kisses,
of glances full of brightness and love.
I will tell you of tears shed,
for a love that is gone,
of the sadness that invades us,
when the heart is broken.
But I will also tell you about happiness,
of those moments that make us vibrate,
of the illusion that makes us dream,
and gives us the strength to fight.
I invite you to follow me on this path,
in which words are the food,
in which emotions are released,
and the heart beats with fervor and feeling.
May my poem awaken something special in you,
a spark that makes you dream,
a memory that makes you smile,
or a tear that makes you remember.
Thus, dear reader, I end my poem,
in the hope of having reached your soul,
and have left an imprint in your heart,

that lasts forever, without any calm.

Pure love

In the silence of the night,
under a sky full of stars,
two souls met,
united in a love without borders.
They looked into each other's eyes,
and they told each other everything without speaking,
their gazes understood each other,
in a language that only they could speak.
Time was flying by,
but they didn't realize it,
because they were lost in their world,
in their love that made them strong.
They loved each other more and more every day,
and that was what made them cry,
because they knew there would be no other love,
that could be as pure as the one they shared.
And so, under the moonlight,
hugged each other tightly,
because they knew that together,
could face any adversity.
Because the love they felt,
was stronger than any storm,
and even if time passed,
their love would continue to glow in the dark.

He did not love me

In the darkness of my soul,
I feel like everything has vanished,
every struggle, every effort, every hope,
has been in vain, all is lost.
The world is collapsing around me,
and I feel like nothing makes sense,
every step I take, every dream I pursue,
seem destined for oblivion.
In that emptiness, in that loneliness,
I thought I had found the light,
a light called love, a light that shone,
but it turned out to be just an illusion.
That person who claimed to love me,
who promised to be by my side at all times,
left when I needed him most,
leaving me alone with my pain and their abandonment.
Now I understand that he never loved me,
that he was only with me for convenience,
that I was never more than an object of their interest,
and that it really meant nothing to her.
Hopelessness embraces me,
pain suffocates me, loneliness eats me up,
and I wonder if I will ever find happiness,
or if my life is destined to be a constant struggle.
But even so, I keep going,
in the hope that someday,
I will find a ray of light in the midst of so much darkness,

and I will be able to dream and believe in life again.

Soul in sorrow

The heart beats with pain and sorrow,
when the moment of separation arrives,
leave the love of your life for an obligation,
and fear never to see his expression again.
Tears well up in sorrowful eyes,
sadness overwhelms and the soul is desolate,
knowing that the game has been decided,
and uncertainty looms like a sword.
The love we leave behind is like a treasure,
that is carried in the deepest part of the heart,
yearning for his presence every day and every hour,
and looking forward to the opportunity to come back soon.
War or threats are cruel situations,
that mercilessly separate us from our loved one,
and even though time passes, the pain remains faithful,
and accompanies us like a shadow in solitude.
It is hard to let go of the love of our life,
because we left a piece of us with him,
and although duty calls, the wound is still open,
and makes us yearn for his presence with great longing.
But despite the pain and sadness we feel,
the love that unites us will never die,
and there will always be a place in our hearts,
for the love we leave behind.

In the shadows of your soul

In the silence of the dark night
the sobs of my soul can be heard
that cries for lost love
and for dreams broken into pieces.
My heart feels empty
like a desert without an oasis
and my mind is a whirlwind
of endless pain and sadness.
Loneliness is my companion
on this aimless road
and the cold of the night embraces me
as a reminder of my pain.
The love I thought was eternal
vanished like smoke
and now I'm left here, alone
with nothing but my pain.
My heart bleeds in silence
and my tears are my comfort
on this heartbreaking night
where pain is my only companion.

What it can do

Love has an unparalleled power
that can transform the darkest soul
and shine the light in the heart
of the most wicked and tenderless being.
Love is like the sun in spring
that awakens the flowers of winter
and gives them the strength to flourish
despite having been in the eternal cold.
Love is capable of rebirth
the tired and hopeless soul
and fill it with life and joy
to believe in the bonanza again.
Love is the guiding force
on the road to happiness
and shows us that even the most evil
can change and find goodness.
Because love has no limits
no borders and no conditions
and can reach into the darkest corners of the world
to illuminate with its warm glow.
So don't lose faith in the power of love.
to change a soul or a heart
because its strength is true and eternal
and can always bring transformation.

An unreal love

Pain brings us closer,
knowing that I will never meet you in person,
hurts in my soul and is felt in my person.
I am poor and I am afraid she will think badly,
that my lack of resources make her judge,
but I can't help but love her,
and meet her through letters in a chat room.
Your words transport me
to a faraway and beautiful place,
where love is possible
and fear has no rest.
Although distance separates us
and fear makes us doubt,
the love I feel for her
is stronger and I can't keep quiet.
So I will continue to write
and dreaming of his presence,
because even if I can't see her in person,
his soul is already part of my existence.
And so, through the letters,
we will continue to build our history,
a love that transcends distance,
and leads us to victory.

Distance

Distance distances us from each other,
but our love does not fade,
we know we will never touch,
but that does not mean that our faith will not grow.
Although sometimes pain invades us,
and loneliness makes us yearn,
we know our love is strong,
and that together we will always be.
Even if our bodies never meet,
our souls unite in an embrace,
and so on, in the distance,
we build a love that never falls apart.
No matter how much time passes,
nor how far we are from each other,
because our love is eternal,
and it will always remain deep inside.
So even if distance separates us,
our love unites us in the same reality,
and so on, in the universe of letters,
we continue to build our happiness.

A wound in the soul

Betrayal is a deep wound,
that mercilessly pierces the soul,
hurts more than a stab wound,
and leaves the heart shattered in loneliness.
When someone you love cheats on you,
and plays with your feelings mercilessly,
you feel as if the world is falling apart,
and the trust you had in that person is gone.
Tears flood your eyes,
and pain consumes your heart,
you ask yourself over and over again why,
and you realize that betrayal is the worst disappointment.
Betrayal is like a dark shadow,
that follows you wherever you go,
and even if you try to forget, the memory lingers,
and the pain and sadness never fully fade away.
But despite all the suffering,
it is important to remember that you are strong,
and that even if betrayal has hurt you,
you have the capacity to love again, to recover.
So don't let betrayal destroy you,
don't let the pain consume you,
always remember that you are brave and powerful,
and that true love always triumphs.

Sadness

I feel the weight of pain in my chest,
a burden that weighs me down and does not leave me alone,
I feel like my soul is in pieces,
and the heart broken into a thousand pieces.
Tears run down my cheeks,
like a river that does not stop,
my body shudders with every sob,
and my mind is lost in a sea of sad memories.
Sadness envelops me like a cold blanket,
and I feel there is no escape,
I feel trapped in a dark labyrinth,
no way out, no light, no hope.
I would like to scream and tear my clothes,
release all the rage and pain inside me,
but the words choke in my throat,
and silence is my only company.
It is difficult to move forward,
when all seems lost,
but I know that at some point,
the sun will shine again in my gray sky.
Until then, I will continue to cry,
releasing the pain that consumes me,
hoping that someday,
find the peace that so longs and consumes me.

Esperanza

Hope is the flame that never goes out,
is the force that drives us forward,
is the engine that drives us to achieve our goals,
and to conquer our biggest and most important dreams.
Hope is the breath that gives us life,
when all seems lost and dark,
is the embrace that comforts us,
when we feel lonely and despondent about the future.
And although there are obstacles and challenges along the way,
nothing can stop us if we have hope in our hearts,
because when we want something with all our strength,
nothing and no one will be able to steal our illusion.
Hope gives us the necessary strength,
to keep going and never give up,
makes us believe that anything is possible,
if we fight bravely and fearlessly.
So, if you have a dream that you want to achieve,
do not lose hope and keep fighting with strength and courage,
because with faith and perseverance,
nothing in this world can stop you from achieving everything
you desire with love.

Eternal enemy

Sometimes the heart asks for love and companionship,
and we long to find someone to share life with,
but the road to love is not always easy,
and sometimes it makes us suffer and fills us with sadness and melancholy.
But even if fear and loneliness invade us,
we must not lose hope of finding true love,
because love is a feeling that completes us and makes us happy,
and is the key that opens the door to a better future.
However, not all of us are born to love,
and sometimes it is better to be alone than in bad company,
because love is a choice and not an obligation,
and it is not fair to force us to love if we do not feel the passion.
It is better to accept loneliness with gratitude and respect,
and enjoy the freedom that being alone gives us,
because life is a road full of ups and downs,
and each one must choose his own path with courage.
So, if love has not yet come into your life,
don't worry or be anxious about being alone,
enjoy your freedom and live every moment with joy,
because happiness does not depend on someone else, but on yourself.

Try

To love is an act of courage,
a leap into the void with no guarantee,
a risk that many are afraid to take,
for fear of being mercilessly hurt.
But love is a beautiful feeling,
able to fill us with joy and happiness,
to make us feel alive and fulfilled,
and to show us the world with gratitude.
Despite this, the fear of love is real,
and the fear of being hurt makes us hesitate,
prevents us from giving ourselves without reserve,
and keeps us away from the happiness we long for.
But we must remember that true love is pure,
there is nothing more powerful in this world,
and although the wound of betrayal may hurt,
it is more painful never to have loved with fervor.
So don't give in to the fear of love,
let your feelings flow unceasingly,
because even though the risk of disappointment is real,
love is the only key that opens the door to happiness.
Remember that love is a gift,
that can only be given with the heart,
and even if we are afraid of being hurt,
it is better to try than to be left with doubt and pain.

Fears

Human fears are dark,
hide in the shadows of the mind,
like an all-encompassing cloud,
dulling the light that makes us live.
Fear of failure paralyzes us,
We are afraid that we will not be up to the task,
and not being able to reach the desired goal,
and be stranded on the shore of life.
Fear of loneliness terrifies us,
we feel that no one wants us around,
and the emptiness in our chest becomes great,
like a black hole that engulfs us.
The fear of death haunts us,
makes us feel vulnerable and helpless,
and the certainty that someday it will come,
shakes us to the core.
And so, the fears of humans,
take us away from what really matters,
leaving us in an abyss of sadness,
not knowing how to escape from that prison.

A tear of farewell

The farewell came with tears in his eyes,
your departure leaving a void in my soul,
I don't know where you're going, what roads you'll travel,
I am afraid of the unknown that awaits you.
Fear eats away at me and makes me tremble,
I don't want to lose what I loved so much,
I clung to you with all my strength,
and now it's hard for me to let go and let you go.
I know you will never return to my side,
that your love now belongs to someone else,
and the pain in my chest does not stop growing,
knowing that another in his body will kiss you.
The thought that of other offshoots will have,
makes me feel like my heart is being ripped out,
and though I know I must let go,
the love I felt for you will always live in me.
So now, with a lump in my throat,
I say goodbye with a broken heart,
hoping that on your way you will find happiness,
and that someday, perhaps, you may forgive my weakness.

Thanks mom

My mother, you are my sunshine
that lights my way
in your arms I find love
that makes me feel like a child.
You are my protective shield
in you I find security
you taught me to be brave
and you never let me fall.
Your love is the purest and most sincere
you never judge me, you always accept me
you are my guide and my inspiration
thank you for being my eternal companion.

Family love

Family is my strength
my refuge in difficult times
in his arms I find comfort
and in his love, the greatest of gifts.
Together, we are a team
that supports each other through thick and thin
we celebrate successes and triumphs
and we get up together from our falls.
In our union we find strength
to overcome any adversity
our love is infinite
and we will always be together in happiness.

Love as a couple

In you I find my happiness
my soul mate, my better half
your love is my greatest treasure
and in your arms I find peace.
Together, we are a perfect team
that is supported at all times
our love is an eternal fire
that keeps us always united.
In your smile I find hope
and in your eyes I see my future
our love is the greatest gift
and will never lose its brightness and brilliance.

Life

Life is an adventure
and love is our guide
in your company I find
the strength to move forward every day.
You are my accomplice in joy
and in sadness my comfort
Your love is my greatest desire
and together, we build our dream.
In your eyes I find peace
that makes me feel complete
in your arms I find love
that fills me completely.

Together, we walk through life
overcoming the obstacles along the way
our love is the strongest
and will never lose its luster and destiny.
I love you with all my being
you are my everything, my sun at dawn
our love is an unparalleled treasure
and will always be present in our home.

50

Thank you

www.ingramcontent.com/pod-product-compliance
Lightning Source LLC
Chambersburg PA
CBHW051355150726

48000CB00003B/1203